THE ULTIMATE GUIDE FOR

WOMEN

ENTREPRENEURS

Dream it. Build it in 2019

CECELIA NOWLIN

Disclaimer

All the material contained in this book is provided for educational and informational purposes only. No responsibility can be taken for any results or outcomes resulting from the use of this material.

While every attempt has been made to provide information that is both accurate and effective, the author does not assume any responsibility for the accuracy or use/misuse of this information.

Table of Contents

INTRODUCTION   v

STARTING A BUSINESS AS A WOMAN   1

HOW TO CREATE YOUR BUSINESS IDEA   3

THE BUSINESS STEPS FOR YOUR BUSINESS
CREATION   5

GOAL SETTING AS A BUSINESS OWNER   7

HOW TO CREATE A BUSINESS PLAN   9

TIME MANAGEMENT AS A WOMAN
ENTREPRENEUR   17

MARKETING STRATEGIES FOR
YOUR BUSINESS   19

DEVELOPING BUSINESS CREDIT   21

FUNDING YOUR BUSINESS   23

TAX EDUCATION FOR BUSINESS OWNERS   29

CONCLUSION   30

ABOUT THE AUTHOR   31

ACKNOWLEDGEMENTS

The names of any people you might want to acknowledge in helping you get this book written. They may be your friends, family members or associates who supported you in the project. You could also mention teachers and people who have inspired you who you might not know personally.

INTRODUCTION

'It's a man's world' or so the saying goes. Being a woman in a patriarchal world is hard enough in a world where women are seen as the 'weaker sex'. Nonetheless, starting a business irrespective of your gender requires share grit, determination and a can-do spirit. Entrepreneurship is not a walk in the park. Entrepreneurship done successfully leads to financial freedom.

This book was written with the aim of helping the 21st helping woman be the best entrepreneur she can be. I hope you enjoy reading it and implementing the tips contained therein as much as I enjoyed writing it.

All the best!

CHAPTER 1

STARTING A BUSINESS AS A WOMAN

A lot more women are starting businesses these days unlike what was obtained in previous centuries. However, entrepreneurship is not as easy as it is made out to be. Realistically, the freedom of having your business as an entrepreneur requires long hours, perseverance and skills to stay afloat in the first few years. In some cases, it requires a team. There is this myth that entrepreneurs have to become one, years after working hard in a company that is not theirs. Some have said that an entrepreneur must first save enough before establishing a small business. There is also the argument that entrepreneurs have to have everything in place before venturing into an enterprise. While preparedness and experience is important, they might not necessarily be the key to being a successful female entrepreneur.

Entrepreneurship is the process of starting a business, typically a startup company by offering an innovative product, process or services. As a woman, there is no special skill that comes with your gender. Entrepreneurship does not discriminate on the sexes which is why men do not have the sole license to succeed at a business. As a woman entrepreneur, it is your duty to perceive an opportunity and exhibit strategies in taking advantage of the opportunity. An entrepreneur is a decision maker, the head of an organization, one who directs, organizes and takes the risks. Also, an entrepreneur is in charge of a team while navigating a ship.

Haven said this, it is clear that entrepreneurship has nothing to do with your gender. You are within your right as a woman to start any business you wish depending on how skilled you are in running the business. While those who have cater for families may find it harder than most to navigate a business, it has been done by women in the past.

There is no right age to start a business. Countless women have started ventures at young and old ages and the business has made good returns. Women can start at any age provided they have the intellect to make a business work. Starting a business as a woman is what you should consider starting- if you haven't already done so.

CHAPTER 2

HOW TO CREATE YOUR BUSINESS IDEA

A business idea details the plan you might have to make a go at a business of your choice. I would advise you to choose a business that best mirrors your passion. Getting inspiration for your business idea can come from daily problems you see people have and want to solve. A successful entrepreneur is one that observes the society, notes the problem in a particular society and brings up workable solutions for them.

Once you discover that you can get ideas from everything in the society, you will realize that ideas are a dime a dozen and you cannot execute them all. This is where a niche becomes important. Instead of trying to solve so many problems at one time, narrow it down to the things you are passionate about. For example, if you love knitting, you might want to consider gathering a group of like-minded people to start a knitting company for babies instead of knitting for everyone. If are passionate about organic food, you might want to consider getting a license to be a dietician for sportsmen instead of everyone. Your business ideas should stem from what you can comfortably do even if the money is not coming in for a few years. Create ideas from your passion and fine-tune the idea with a business coach.

CHAPTER 3

THE BUSINESS STEPS FOR YOUR BUSINESS CREATION

C reating business steps for your business creation requires strategy. These steps are crucial for every woman who wishes to be an entrepreneur. These steps will serve as a guide to prevent you from making costly mistakes and minimizing risks to the barest minimum. With these steps, you can work out business strategies that will serve as a blueprint for your entrepreneurship venture.

Identify your passion and a problem that lies within the industry

- Each industry or niche has a unique problem that needs to be solved. Research what others in the industry are doing and what unique value proposition you can bring to the table in solving that problem.

Outline your business strategy

- Your business strategy is the sum of all the activities you plan to undertake towards the actualization of your business goals. These strategies are calculated and informed moves made towards making the best business decisions. Before you come up with a strategy for your business, it is expedient to set up business goals.

Set goals and execute them

- In the next chapter, we will talk about setting business goals and executing them in detail. Goals are meant to serve as a compass for what your business wants to achieve and how best it can be executed.

CHAPTER 4

GOAL SETTING AS A BUSINESS OWNER

Goal setting is essential for any business. Developing goals are crucial because business goals are established to approach entrepreneurship with the right information, strategy and plan. Goals serve as a blueprint that reminds you of the bigger picture. It gives you a focus point. Business goals provide the motivation to carry on even when inspiration is low.

Choosing and registering a business is one of the first things you should consider doing as an entrepreneur. A business name is an identity. It is the name by which your company will be known for and a lasting feature of your brand. Picking out a name for the business sets things in motion and calls the business to life. Ensure that the business name you are selecting is not in existence. A little online search can help you eliminate any problems that might arise from this. A neutral name is usually advisable although some people want their business to be a reflection of themselves and they end of giving the business their own names.

No matter your decision, ensure that the business is duly registered while matching the kind of business description it is to portray. Set business goals for yourself in the next few weeks but a review should be done after every month until things take full shape.

CHAPTER 5

HOW TO CREATE A BUSINESS PLAN

Business plans are the overall vision of the business and the timeline by which they will be achieved. When starting a business, start with the basics and take it one step after the other.

The business plan of every startup should include your mission, a set of business goals you want to achieve and the vision statement. It should also include reasons that are attainable, and plans for reaching them. Also, it may include background and details about the team and founders. Business plans may include branding and marketing strategies, visibility studies and long term goals. A few pages should be enough to say everything needed to say. Business plans may cover the development of your startup and the structuring of the organization. Business plans identify and target internal goals, but provide only general guidance on how they will be met are called strategic plans.

Business plans should not be long, full of irrelevant details or out of date. Be precise and summarize all the information in a few pages. In fact, today a business plan may be easily summarized in a power point deck together with an excel model that includes the following slides:

1. Introduction

Who are you? Keep it short.

2. Team

Show the person(s) behind the idea and briefly describe the role.

3. Problem

What problem are you trying to solve? Is it really a problem?

4. Advantages

What makes your solution special? How are you different from others?

5. Solution

Describe how you are planning to solve the problem.

6. Product

How does your product or service actually work? Show some examples.

7. Traction

Traction means having a measurable set of customers that serves to prove a potential.

8. Market

Know, or at least attempt to predict, the size of your target market.

9. Competition

What are the alternative solutions to the problem you are trying to solve?

10. Business model

How are you planning to make money? Show a schedule when you expect revenues to pour in.

11. Investing

What is your planned budget? What kind of money are you looking for?

12. Contact

Leave your contact details and let people know how to reach you quickly.

A business plan will should have S.M.A.R.T goals

A business plan should have realistic and S.M.A.R.T goals. Setting defined business goals means having an action plan from the beginning to end of the business journey. These business goals should be S.M.A.R.T (specified, measurable, achievable, realistic and with a time frame). All this should be done within a specified time frame or any other time frame you choose to achieve the set goals.

Start with a defined line of action and be disciplined about it. S.M.A.R.T. goals help those who are at a loss on what constitutes a good business plan. With the guideline, your goals are clear and concise. This way, your chances of success are also higher. When a goal is SMART, it provides an unencumbered framework for defining and managing set goals and objectives.

As a female entrepreneur, the questions below serve as a SMART model guideline in setting up your business:

Specific

- What is the exact accomplishment I want achieved within in this business? What is the overall goal of the business? Writing and naming the specified task is more effective than when making a general goal.

- If you were not to get an investor, why would the person be interested in this business? As an investor, who will be involved in this business?

- How much have I set aside to venture into this business?

- Do I have the necessary skills and know-how to be an entrepreneur?

- What is the aim of going into this business?

- Where do I want my office to be? Will I work from home? Any particular location that best works best for the intending business? Can the business survive in this area? Who are the competitors in this niche and how can I bring a unique and fresh perspective to the niche?

- When: What is the time frame necessary to get the right certification needed in penetrating this kind of market? What are the constraints? Can they be surmounted during the allotted time frame?

- What are the specific reasons for starting the business and the benefits attached to accomplishing the set goals and at the right time?

- Are my plans tasks specific? For example, if you want to have a natural hair care line, a specific goal is starting a course to learn different textures of hair and a license to start operating.

Measurable

By setting measurable action plans and tasks, you establish concrete criteria for measuring the progress of set goals. By measuring the progress of the set goals, the goals are on track and the timeline followed to the latter. Targets are met, deadlines are reached and everything falls into place with the set target. Measurements of goals need to be in line with set goals. Measurable answers the question: How will I know when it is accomplished?

Attainable

When set business goals are attainable, they are easily achieved within the set period. If you want to start a business that involves a license do well to get that out of the way as soon as you can because it usually takes longer.

With the right documents and the right information, you can get start your business even from the comfort of your home. For a goal to be attainable, arrange them in order of importance and identify business goals that are most important. When this has been achieved, figure out to stick to the timeline. Develop the attitudes, abilities, skills and financial capacity to reach your goals.

All goals are achievable. You can achieve almost any goal you set your mind to if you plan your steps wisely and establish a time frame that allows you to carry out those steps. Business goals require time, strategy and careful planning to be achieved. Things that seem insurmountable eventually seem inconsequential not because your goals shrink but because you are determined to achieve them because you know they are doable.

Nevertheless, your expertise and knowledge must match these goals. Without the right knowledge, it is impossible to set goals and attain them. Your goals are usually proportionate to the knowledge of your subject matter and it is only when you gain the right knowledge about real estate investing can you set goals that are specific, measurable and achievable.

Realistic

A realistic goal is one that is achievable during the set period. The higher the chances of this goal being done before by another individual in the same field, the better your chances. For example, if you want to open a lemonade store, what are the estimated returns on the business?

Are these returns realistic? Let's say you want to invest in a clothing brand worth $100, 000 dollars but you want the returns a week later. Is this a realistic goal? I'm afraid not. Is it possible to get your business properly established within a month? If yes, do you have the right information and network to properly market and gain grounds? That's a question only you can honestly answer.

A realistic goal should not be impossible to attain for the individual who set it. Personalize your goals as much as possible. The whole essence of a realistic goal (key word here being realistic) is that it is within your power to achieve. Other exploits can be a motivating factor that reflects your decision but it should never be the yardstick by which your goals are measured. A realistic goal must represent an objective toward which you are both willing and able to work. A goal can be both high and realistic but you are the only one who can decide just how high your goal should be.

Each goal is a step closer to the overall journey and each step should be seen as progress.

Time-bound

A goal should always have a time frame. In the next chapter, we will talk about time management in depth especially for those who run families while planning to run a business. For time bound goals, they put a particular goal achievable within a time frame. When no time frame is tied to your projects, there is a high likelihood of procrastination because the goals are unattached to any sense of urgency. Playing the "someday" game is detrimental. Put things in motion and let your mind adapt to this date.

CHAPTER 6

TIME MANAGEMENT AS A WOMAN ENTREPRENEUR

Time is a crucial factor when it comes to entrepreneurship. Time can be the difference between making a sale and losing an opportunity. As an entrepreneur, you need to learn how to manage your time so that it does not interfere in other activities. Most women are still caregivers and makers of the home hence entrepreneurship is something they have to combine with family.

When it comes to entrepreneurship, you have to make time even when it is not convenient. As women, your days might be saddled with so many things and more often than not, you are busy. 24 hours doesn't seem just enough to accomplish all the things set for the day. There are bills to pay, meetings to attend, children to cater for and passion to purpose.

Getting a calendar or writing down your schedule helps to manage your time so as to get work done because really, entrepreneurship involves work. You can also use Google calendar or apps that help with coordination and daily time planning. A daily planner or a to-do list with the exact time for set tasks helps you achieve more within a day.

If you want to succeed at a business, you have to do the work, make time, limit screen time, be positive and above all, get started instead of procrastinating.

Get a to-do list. Write down three things you do every day and make the most of your time. For example, what three things can I do today that will help me get make headway in my business? Can I substitute my TV time to go over my finances? What can I sacrifice to make sure I go over my business daily? Do I see less TV, less binging or find time to work out between office hours? Find time.

CHAPTER 7

MARKETING STRATEGIES FOR YOUR BUSINESS

A s a case study, we shall use 18-24 months as a period of business plan, where you need to get all resources required. Your goal is to maintain hype and momentum of the business and create marketing buzz around it. Use these key points to create marketing strategies for your business.

Market risk

- Are there customers for your product? How can you evidence that?

- Who needs your product and will why will they choose it over alternative solutions?

Technical risk

- Can it be made at scale?

- And can it be made at a cost which makes it competitive with alternatives?

Team risk

- Do you and your team have the necessary skills?

- Can you execute and bring this idea to the market better than competing teams? Are you good enough?

Don't forget that delivering value and reaching sales for products remain key components of being a woman entrepreneur. Ensure your marketing game is topnotch. Your short term marketing goals should center on the following:

- How can my startup penetrate the market in these allocated months and through what mediums?

- Will enough people buy this product?

- Can they afford it? Will they be willing and able to pay and for how much?

Start by creating a prototype of your product and focus on getting an actual client first.

Marketing and sales are integral parts of a business if not the core. There should be a strong focus on marketing from the beginning. As an entrepreneur you need to know where your customer really is. You need to get facts from them and develop strategies to win them over. Selling and creative marketing tips are fundamental skills that any founder need to develop at the very beginning; you need to truly work on those from the onset.

CHAPTER 8

DEVELOPING BUSINESS CREDIT

B alance your credit cards so you can have the opportunity to raise your credit scores. While your bank wants you to always carry a balance on your credit card, so they can collect the interest, they also don't want you to have too high of a balance. The reason paying down your credit cards can increase your score so quickly is because of something known as "Utilization ratio" on revolving debts. A "Utilization ratio" is simply the amount of debt you own on any particular revolving debt divided into the total credit limit. For example, if you have a card with a $10,000 limit and you currently owe $6,000 on that card, divide the $6,000 balance into the $10,000 limit and you will come up with a utilization ratio of 60%. It is important to understand how this affects your scores in the first place. Utilization ratios account for approximately 30% of your FICO score, which is almost one third of your entire score. While your bank wants you to carry a balance so they can collect the interest payments, they also don't want you carrying a high balance in relation to the limit. The general rule is to never owe more than 30% of the limit.

You may be thinking of flipping your card and saving yourself some interest but you are doing major damage to your scores. By constantly flipping from card to card, you are decreasing the average age of your open accounts. My advice is to avoid the debt in the first place. If you find yourself in a place where you "have to" constantly carry large amounts of credit card debt than you need to take a hard look at your lifestyle and see what is causing this to be a constant.

Having a great credit score is simply insurance in case something terrible happens to your business. You probably have insurance on your car, house, life and health. Why would you not have insurance for your business? You need to be sure that you don't have to burn through your savings and start over on your nest egg.

Having and maintaining a good business credit is not difficult. Read the fine print and study your credit report properly.

CHAPTER 9

FUNDING YOUR BUSINESS

O ften times, we hear stories about entrepre-
neurs-male and female- go around with their
proposals from door to door and investor to
investor begging for an opportunity. Enthusiasm is not
enough. No investor wants to hear how many nights you
have been up thinking of the perfect prototype for your
business model. They need visible results.

While some of these disappointments go ahead to
spur these entrepreneurs to make it work without funding, it doesn't always end up on a positive note. Most investors will not believe in you until you make that start-up
something worth associating with. You may believe in
your business but it takes a lot of convincing to make
someone believe in you. You need to build that trust over
time.

It is important to do some homework about the kind
of investors you need as an entrepreneur. Most entrepre-

neurs do not know this and will still go ahead to ask for funding from someone who has absolutely no interest in their vision. What kind of businesses do they invest in? Do they champion women causes? What drives their business decisions? You have to do a true due diligence on them because it makes a very different impact on the investor if you send them a note and tell them that you know exactly the kind of companies they invest in and why yours fit the profile. Also, you have to try to get introduced adequately to the investor and learn in advance from him and from other people he has invested in.

Don't take things personal and get demotivated when investors do not share your business enthusiasm and energy. It might not even be because of your gender. It is your idea and it depends solely on you to sell them your vision and make them see what you are seeing. You always have to maintain an extraordinary level of enthusiasm no matter if funding is available or not.

Not all businesses need external funding. There are some startups that require basic things that a few dollars can take care of, thereby making external funding unnecessary. The main idea here is that your best investor is a customer. The second main idea here is that a lot of companies need capital, but not a lot of companies need venture capital, which is a very special kind of capital that demands very high returns in a limited time.

Not all businesses start small but indeed, all businesses should. It gives the start-up the chance to take a breather and go through its ups and downs. It also gives the entrepreneur the chance to be the sole CEO of his startup even though he will bear the whole risk involved by bootstrapping. When you match this with limited sales and marketing costs, you will see that you may not need external funding for your project.

Let's say you decide to start a publishing company, these are some of the things you will need are as follows: A printer, a computer, a space (you can decide to start from your home), some inks and an internet connection (this is optional). With these items, you are more than ready to go. While customers many take time to give you their loyalty, these basic needs should be covered by your savings. If you have a similar business model, you do not need to worry about external start-up funds. All you need to do is develop a solid plan and focus your energy on growing your start-up.

For some entrepreneurs, external funding is the only option. The question is to ask these fundamental questions:

- When will I need the subsequent influx of money?

- How will I deploy this capital? What will I achieve with this money and the subsequent one?

- Where will I get it? From which source will secure the cash I need to get this project running?

If you can effectively answer these effectively, then your work is getting easier even though you do not realize it.

Other Funding Options

There are other funding options available when investors delay. They are:

Bootstrapping:

All entrepreneurs should bootstrap initially. This involves little drops of funds gotten from family, savings, friends and well-wishers. When you pitch your idea to your close contacts to raise funding, you must explain the plan in detail, the pros and cons and how you plan to make money and sustain the startup. Most of this money may not be seen as loans since they are from family unless otherwise specified. Your business model, strategies and your overall business plan should be focused on organic approach and base minimum expenses.

Grants/Government Loans:

In some countries, there are organizations that go out of their way to provide loans and grants to entrepreneurs in conjunction with the government or with private funds. There are also grants available or strictly women entrepreneurs. You may want to look up your country's policies for this. In some cases, there is the option to apply for a grant or seek for government funded loans. Government often releases policies to develop socio-economic causes. If you are looking to raise funding via this means, your plan must comply with the policy regulations. It is also imperative that your business plan establishes an adequate socio-economic development for the people in and around the geography you are planning to start. Also look up those who have benefitted from past grants to have an insight on the subject.

Bank Loans:

Majority of bank loans for businesses are based on collaterals. If you don't have collateral to offer, forget this mode of funding. Nevertheless, you can structure your capital requirements with a combination of bank loan and other investment modes based on the business model. Your business plan for a bank loan must substantiate the ability to pay off the loan raised along with its interest. Go over these requirements with an investment banker or lawyer if you do not understand some terminologies.

Angels:

Angels invest in your venture in exchange of equity. The capital requirement usually ranges up to 2 m and they expect a 10 to 20 times return over a period of 5 to 7 years. There are two kinds of angel funding possible. More popular kind is the one where the angel is looking for an exit either by management buyout or dilution in the future round of funding. The other kind which is rare, works as an active partner with you on the venture. The business plan focused towards an angel must have research to substantiate your venture and clear long term financial goals.

Venture Capitalists:

VCs usually aim at having a portfolio of ventures and each VC firm has their sweet spot for investment. You must research your investor in details before approaching them and tweak your business plan to ensure it matches what they are looking for. Valuations play an important role in VC funding. Your business plan should also visualize your scale up process clearly along with future funding requirements.

Private Equity:

PE's are not exactly an entrepreneur's first option. PE's usually do not invest in startups. They look for mature businesses. If you are approaching PEs you must have your previous financials in your business plan along with your growth plans which relates to your previous financials.

CHAPTER 10

TAX EDUCATION FOR BUSINESS OWNERS

G et the necessary tax education for your business by walking into your local tax office to make enquiries. Fill in your tax paper work early or get an accountant or expert to do this.

Declaring taxes are very important for any entrepreneur. Avoiding taxes can land you in jail especially if they are undeclared. Ensure your tax paperwork is up to date.

CONCLUSION

It is my fervent hope that this ultimate guide for women entrepreneurs inspires you to do more as a woman and as an entrepreneur. Entrepreneurship is not exclusive to one gender. Entrepreneurs make tough choices and pay the price so that generations yet unborn will live in financial freedom. The female gender is not an impediment to entrepreneurship. It is an asset. Every great step begins with a decision. Once people decide that they will be the instrument of change in their families and communities, they will be open to taking business risks and doing daring exploits irrespective of what society thinks of them.

ABOUT THE AUTHOR

Cecelia Nowlin is the owner & founder of Empower Business Group. She is a public speaker, business coach and author of the new book 'The Ultimate Guide For Women Entrepreneurs'. This book teaches women about entrepreneurship and her first popular book 'Business Basics 101' the business foundation for start-ups. Cecelia's journey started about 12 years ago. She hated her job and wanted her freedom. She went to the courthouse and got her DBA. She was excited. She realized at that moment she had no idea how to start her business from there. Through that experience, and through trial and error, she built multiple successful businesses from the ground up. Her recent book "The Ultimate Guide for Women Entrepreneurs" originally came from her experience as a woman entrepreneur.